MW00917340

One-Minute Prayers® for Girls

HARVEST
kids™

HARVEST HOUSE PUBLISHERS
EUGENE, OREGON

Cover design by Dugan Design Group

ONE-MINUTE PRAYERS is a registered trademark of The Hawkins Children's LLC. Harvest House Publishers, Inc., is the exclusive licensee of the federally registered trademark ONE-MINUTE PRAYERS.

HARVEST KIDS is a registered trademark of The Hawkins Children's LLC. Harvest House Publishers, Inc., is the exclusive licensee of the federally registered trademark HARVEST KIDS.

ONE-MINUTE PRAYERS® FOR GIRLS

Copyright © 2018
Published by Harvest House Publishers
Eugene, Oregon 97408
www.harvesthousepublishers.com

ISBN 978-0-7369-7346-5 (cloth)
ISBN 978-0-7369-7347-2 (eBook)

Printed in China

18 19 20 21 22 23 24 25 26 / RDS-CD / 10 9 8 7 6 5 4 3 2

Contents

What Is Prayer?

You need special skills to play on a soccer team or dance in a ballet or perform in a band concert. But did you know you don't need any special skills to pray? It's true! You don't need to know the Bible backward and forward. You don't have to have a big vocabulary. You don't need to be good at speaking in front of a group. All you need is a desire to connect with God.

If you can have a conversation with a brother or a sister or a parent or a friend, you can have a conversation with God. And that is what prayer is all about—having a conversation with God. Did you know that talking to God is actually easier than talking to people? When you're talking to Him, He never interrupts you or takes your words the wrong way or misunderstands you. God knows you so well, He understands what you want to tell Him—even when you might not totally understand it yourself!

Prayer is simple. But prayer is also powerful. Having a conversation with God about the things that matter most in your life—your friends, your family, your future, your faith—can change you and everything around you in amazing and exciting ways.

Ready to make prayer a part of your life? Let's dig in and get that conversation going and start connecting with God!

Prayers About
God and Me

Simple

LORD my God, I called to you for help,
and you healed me.

PSALM 30:2

Dear God...

What would happen if I were to take a test on everything I could ever possibly know? Every math problem ever created. Every science question in the world. Every language spoken on the planet. Every spelling word—ever. I'm freaking out just thinking about it. There's no way I would pass. There's no way anyone would pass—even the smartest person in the world!

Thankfully, prayer isn't like that. It might seem complicated, like there's a definite right and wrong way to pray, but it's actually very simple. And I will never fail when I pray. The main thing I need to remember is this: I talk to You, God, and You hear me. Then You answer, and I listen for Your response. That's it! Conversation between You and me. Easy. Uncomplicated. Simple. Thank You for that.

Amen.

Today

Do not worry about tomorrow,
for tomorrow will worry about itself.

MATTHEW 6:34

Dear God...

What do You have planned for me today? Who are the people I'm going to talk to and spend time with? What will they teach me, and what will I share with them? What things are going to happen, and how am I going to react to those things? Help me to react to people and situations in a good way. If I don't know what to say or how to respond, remind me to turn to You for help.

I want to focus on living each day in the best way I can. Sometimes I spend too much time looking ahead. I think things will be better when I'm older or in a different situation. But You have amazing plans for my life right now—on this very day.

Amen.

Unsure

I will instruct you and teach you in the
way you should go;
I will counsel you with my
loving eye on you.

PSALM 32:8

Dear God...

Who should I eat lunch with? Which gymnastics level is going to be the right one for me? Should I sign up for just one week of summer camp, or would I be okay being away from home for two or more weeks?

Sometimes I feel so unsure of what to do. I like making decisions for myself, but it can be easier if someone else makes them for me. Yet I know it's important for me to learn to make good choices on my own. I'm glad I don't really have to make these choices by myself. Lord, You are always there to hold my hand and guide me in every decision. In the moments when I am undecided and unsure, I can always seek Your guidance and Your truth.

Amen.

Wise

The LORD gives wisdom;
from his mouth come knowledge
and understanding.

PROVERBS 2:6

Dear God...

Sometimes I wish I could know how something will turn out in the end. If I had known I would get the role I wanted in the play, auditioning would have been a breeze. If I had known the new girl next door would end up as my best friend, I wouldn't have been so nervous to talk to her. And if I had known I was going to break my leg, I probably wouldn't have played soccer that day!

Only You know what's going to happen though, Lord. And maybe that's a good thing. You want me to try new things and to talk to new people. I can trust You because You love me and You are wise. Your love and wisdom can get me through anything—even if it isn't what I was expecting.

Amen.

Pray

Pray in the Spirit on all occasions
with all kinds of prayers and requests.

EPHESIANS 6:18

Dear God...

I know there is no one right way to pray, but as I get older and talk to You more and more, I'm figuring out the ways I prefer to pray. I know that You want my prayers to be specific with plenty of details. You want to know what's really going on in my heart. And You want me to share everything with You—things about my friends and my life and my feelings.

I used to think of prayer as just a wish list for myself and other people. I know it's fine to ask You for things, but there's also way more to it than that. When I approach You in prayer, it's like approaching my very best friend. I'm ready to share, and I'm prepared to listen.

Amen.

Listen

Consider carefully what you hear...
With the measure you use, it will be
measured to you—and even more.

MARK 4:24

Dear God...

Talking to anyone can be scary. I don't want to say something I don't mean or have my words come out wrong. This can happen even when I'm praying—especially when I have to pray out loud. Suddenly I find myself thinking only about the words I'm saying, and I forget I'm saying them to You.

During moments when I'm too focused on my own words, help me to stop and listen. Quiet my mind and my heart. Shift my focus to Your awesomeness. Encourage me to just relax and spend time in Your presence, hanging out with You. It's not about my words. It's about You and Your Word.

Amen.

Fear

You who fear the LORD, praise him!

PSALM 22:23

Dear God...

I'll admit I'm afraid of some people. That coach who likes to yell. My friend's mom who always seems upset. The mean kid in my class who never says anything nice to anyone. I'm careful around these people, and I don't usually feel happy when they're nearby.

When I read in the Bible that I should fear You, Lord, help me to remember this is a different kind of fear. Maybe a better word than "fear" would be "respect." You aren't going to get mad at me or yell at me or be mean to me. You always want the best for me, and so I will fear You in a good way—with thankfulness and respect for Your power. You're on my side.

Amen.

Care

He will not let your foot slip—
he who watches over you will not slumber.

PSALM 121:3

Dear God...

When someone tells me You are watching me, I get a mental image of You ready to catch me doing something wrong. I know You see everything I do—right or wrong—but there's a better way for me to think about You.

Instead of seeing You as the one who will catch me misbehaving or messing up, it's better for me to see You as the one who will keep me in Your care. You have given me guidelines and rules to follow so that I will remain safe and protected from anything that might harm me. Because I love You and trust You, the image of You watching me is a good image. You keep me in Your care.

Amen.

Humble

Be completely humble and gentle;
be patient, bearing with
one another in love.

EPHESIANS 4:2

Dear God...

I'm sure I've shouted "Me first!" before. And I feel as if I've heard those words shouted a million times. It's how we guarantee we get a turn playing the game or the first pick of dessert or the best place in line.

One of Your characteristics, God, is that You are humble. You put others first. You focus on what is best for us. You don't step on us because You are God. And You want us to act the same way toward others. When I'm feeling impatient or wanting to get ahead, help me to remember this. Show me the rewards of a humble spirit, and give me Your contentment when I say, "No, you can go first."

Amen.

Church

Where two or three gather in my name, there I am with them.

MATTHEW 18:20

Dear God...

Sometimes I don't want to go to church. Sleeping in sounds better. Wearing my pajamas all day is preferable to putting on nice clothes. Or sometimes I procrastinate all weekend and put off doing my homework until Sunday. Besides, it seems like my family is always stressed out and in a hurry to eat breakfast and make it to church on time.

When I'm feeling this way, please remind me of all the good things that happen when I attend church. I get to hang out with friends who are following You. I learn new things about You. I experience the awesome power of praying together. In the end, it's always worth it, and I'm always glad I went. Help me to remember that going to church is always the best way to spend my Sunday morning.

Amen.

Light

*This is the message we have heard from
him and declare to you: God is light;
in him there is no darkness at all.*

1 John 1:5

Dear God...

When I try to find my way around my house in the dark, I stumble and run into things and get totally mixed up and turned around. Even my bedroom, which I know so well, seems completely different in the dark. But when I turn on a light, everything becomes clear. Suddenly the space is familiar again, and I know where to go.

The same thing happens when I try to live my life without Your light, Lord. I run into problems. I can't make sense of things. I get so mixed up and turned around that I can't get anything right. Yet the solution is so simple. Read Your Word. Talk to You. Spend time in Your presence. Turn on the light.

Amen.

Habit

In the morning, LORD, you hear my voice;
in the morning I lay my requests before you
and wait expectantly.

PSALM 5:3

Dear God...

I've read that we have to do something for 21 days in a row before it becomes a habit. And anything can become a habit. I get used to making my bed every morning, and when I don't, it looks weird. I practice getting up at the same time every morning until I get used to it. I take my vitamins every day at breakfast, and suddenly it's no big deal.

So I guess the secret to making something a habit is...doing it. Consistently. Every day. That's why I need to put effort into reading my Bible and praying. Lord, I want to spend time with You every day. I want it to feel weird when I *don't* do those things. The most important thing in my life is You, so help me to make spending time with You a habit.

Amen.

Prayers About
My Family

Mistakes

God is our refuge and strength,
an ever-present help in trouble.

PSALM 46:1

Dear God...

When I was little, my parents and my teachers praised me when I learned to do something all by myself. And I still get a happy feeling when I finally accomplish something with no help at all. *I did it!* I tell myself.

Sometimes, though, I'm a little too eager to show my independence. I'm excited to grow up, but occasionally I'll do something that goes against what my parents want me to do. When I strike out on my own without listening to them, I often make mistakes. I'm so thankful that You—and my parents—are there for me when I try to do too much. A healthy dose of independence is good, but it's also important to get help when I need it.

Amen.

Seeing

As water reflects the face,
so one's life reflects the heart.

PROVERBS 27:19

Dear God...

My parents and I have been experiencing some tension recently. We don't see things the same way. I feel like they don't understand my life, and they feel like I'm not understanding their concerns about me. We try to talk about the problems, but sometimes our words come out wrong and we end up even more upset with each other.

I want things to go back to the way they used to be, but I don't like to feel misunderstood. Jesus, help me to remember that my parents want the best for me and that their job is to love me and protect me. When I'm trying to explain things to them, help me to keep my heart open to what they—and You—are trying to teach me. Help me to see things from their viewpoint.

Amen.

Sorry

*Confess your sins to each other and
pray for each other so that you may
be healed. The prayer of a righteous
person is powerful and effective.*

JAMES 5:16

Dear God...

It can be so hard to say two little words: "I'm
sorry." And it can be even harder to mean what I
say. Sometimes I just don't feel sorry. I'm still mad
at my brother. Or annoyed with my sister. Or frustrated with my mom and dad. But when I hurt
someone with my words or actions, I'm expected
to say I'm sorry. So I say it.

Then a funny thing happens. After I say the
words, I actually do feel a little bit sorry. And I'm
not quite as mad or annoyed or frustrated. Before
I know it, I really *am* sorry. I might even smile or
laugh. There is so much power in an apology. It
makes others feel better, and it makes me feel better. Please help me to say those two little words—
"I'm sorry."

Amen.

Peace

Make every effort to live in peace
with everyone and to be holy; without
holiness no one will see the Lord.

HEBREWS 12:14

Dear God...

I don't like it when my home isn't peaceful. My parents sometimes argue. My siblings fight. Or we're all upset with each other and everyone's yelling. Maybe I yell back. Maybe I go hide in my room. Maybe I start crying. I want everyone to be happy and get along, but that doesn't always happen.

Lord, even if I can't understand the reasons my home isn't peaceful, help me to turn to You when my stomach hurts and I can't stop my tears. Nobody's family is ever perfect, and no individual is ever perfect—except You. You have given me Your promise that You will always take care of me and that I will be okay if I turn to You. Help me to trust that You will bring peace to my life and my family.

Amen.

Embarrassing

Honor your father and your mother,
so that you may live long in the land
the LORD your God is giving you.

EXODUS 20:12

Dear God...

My parents can be sooo embarrassing! It seems like the older I get, the more I have to worry about what they will say or do. Fortunately, my friends are dealing with the same thing. Do parents think it's part of the job description to embarrass their kids? To be honest, sometimes I wish I could hide them— or make them invisible!

When I really think about it, though, my parents are pretty awesome. Even if what they wear is kind of weird or the things they say sound super silly, I know they love me. They take care of me. They teach me about You. If I can just remember not to care quite so much about how they look or sound, we can actually have a pretty good time together.

Amen.

Mini-Me

*Follow my example, as I follow
the example of Christ.*

1 Corinthians 11:1

Dear God...

Sometimes people comment that I look just
like my brother or sister or mom or dad, but I think
I look like myself. My sister and I might have the
same eyes, and my dad and I might have the same
smile, but each of us is our own person. Sometimes
it's fun to be called a Mini-Me, but sometimes I just
want to be *me*.

The coolest thing to know is that I'm a Mini-Me
of You, God. You created me in Your own image,
and when I think of how powerful and creative
and loving You are, I'm amazed. When it comes to
comparing myself to You, Lord, I should always feel
proud and happy. I'm Your Mini-Me. It's a lot to live
up to, but it's totally worth it.

Amen.

Compare

*Each one should test their own
actions. Then they can take pride in
themselves alone, without comparing
themselves to someone else.*

GALATIANS 6:4-5

Dear God...

You have made me a unique person, but I still get compared to my brother. Or my sister. Or even my cousin. Sometimes I do the comparing myself. I'm a better athlete, but he's a better student. She's a better singer, but I'm a better dancer. The problem with this comparing is that it always ends up with someone feeling less than or not good enough.

Jesus, help me to remember that You made all of us good enough—more than good enough, in fact! And You don't compare us. You have a relationship with every person individually. What's between You and me is just that—between You and me. Just thinking about that already makes me feel better about myself and proud to be who You created me to be.

Amen.

Laugh

Our mouths were filled with laughter,
our tongues with songs of joy.

PSALM 126:2

Dear God...

My family and I have some of the best times together when we're laughing so hard that our tummies hurt and tears roll out of our eyes. You know, the kind of laughter that makes you spit out the water you just tried to drink. All-out giggles and screams of delight.

Lord, thank You for giving me a fun family. We share inside jokes and can get each other laughing with just a funny face. We might look crazy to other people, but we also look like a lot of fun. You created us with a sense of humor, and You expect us to use it. Thank You for the gift of laughter and a silly family that can smile in any situation.

Amen.

Others

Do nothing out of selfish ambition or vain conceit. Rather, in humility value others above yourselves, not looking to your own interests but each of you to the interests of others.

PHILIPPIANS 2:3-4

Dear God...

When I have a big performance or playoff game or a birthday, it's easy for me to consider myself the most important person in my family. Even if I don't intend to be selfish, sometimes it just happens. I put my own needs above the needs of my siblings or parents. And once I start doing that, it becomes a hard habit to break.

That's not how You created families to work, though, God. If everyone thinks they are number one, nobody will help or listen or be there for anyone else. Remind me to focus on the other members of my family instead of just myself. Show me ways to love them and care for them as only I can.

Amen.

Home

*Whatever you do, work at it with all
your heart, as working for the Lord.*

COLOSSIANS 3:23

Dear God...

I don't usually put a lot of thought into my home. Sometimes it's messy and sometimes it's clean, but I'm used to most things being taken care of for me. Sure, I do my chores—I load the dishwasher and fold the laundry and try to keep my room somewhat clean. But I don't put much thought into the big things.

When I scatter my stuff around or forget to do my chores, it affects everyone in my family. But when I do my part to pick up the mess—and maybe a little extra—my home looks so much nicer. And everyone else has a little less work to do, which means more time for play and family togetherness. Lord, You created us to help each other. Help me remember to do my part.

Amen.

Hospitality

Offer hospitality to one another without grumbling.

1 Peter 4:9

Dear God...

When I see my dad making coffee for his small group or my mom offering eggs from our chickens to the neighbors, I'm catching little glimpses of hospitality. I'm seeing what it means to make others feel welcome in my life, to share freely without worrying if the house is messy or the food is perfect or everything is just right.

Practicing hospitality is like saying, "Won't you come in? Welcome into my life." That's how You want all of us to live, Lord. Opening our doors and sharing what we have and caring more about friendship than image. Even at my age, I can learn to practice hospitality when I accept others and share what I have with my family and friends.

Amen.

Jesus

*Dear children, let us not love with words
or speech but with actions and in truth.*

1 JOHN 3:18

Dear God...

When I hear about showing Your love to others,
I usually think of being kind to friends or strangers.
But what about my own family? Even if they are
the ones who taught me about You, I can still show
Your love to them. In fact, it's important for me to
treat my family the way You treat me.

You are patient with me. You are kind to me. You
are faithful to me. Because these things are true, I
need to be patient with my family. I need to be kind
to them. And I need to be faithful to them. Please
make me like You so that everyone—including my
family—can see You in my attitude and actions.

Amen.

No

If you love me, keep my commands.
John 14:15

Dear God...

My parents say no when it seems like everyone else's parents say yes. It can be really frustrating when my mom or dad won't let me do something or have something. It's hard feeling as if I'm the only one, as if I'm all alone. *Why me?* I wonder.

During these times, God, please help me to remember I'm not the only one. Other kids have parents who say no too. Maybe they say no to different things, but they still say no. And saying no can actually be a way of saying yes. Yes, I love you. Yes, I understand that you aren't ready for this. Yes, I care about you. Help me to accept their "no" as proof of their love for me.

Amen.

Waiting

*Those who [wait on] the LORD will renew
their strength. They will soar on wings
like eagles; they will run and not grow
weary, they will walk and not be faint.*

ISAIAH 40:31

Dear God...

A lot of family time seems to be spent waiting.
Waiting for a younger sibling to catch up. Waiting
until I'm old enough to do something. Waiting for
people to get ready so we can get going on our next
adventure. Waiting isn't fun. It's often boring—
especially when it seems like everyone else is slower
than I am.

I can learn lessons by waiting though. I can
start reading a book. Or drawing a picture. Or I can
just be still and talk to You, Lord. When I wait, I'm
accepting that I'm a part of something bigger, that
it's not all about me. Waiting helps me develop
patience and thoughtfulness. Waiting helps me to
see the world in a new light. Waiting can be good.

Amen.

Prayers About
My Friends

Endings

See, I am doing a new thing!
Now it springs up; do you not perceive it?
I am making a way in the wilderness
and streams in the wasteland.

ISAIAH 43:19

Dear God...

One of the hardest things in the world is when a friendship ends. Like when a best friend lives right next door but then moves to a different state. Or a girl I always hang out with in gymnastics suddenly stops talking to me. Or maybe I am the one who ends a friendship. We just didn't seem to have much in common anymore, and I didn't feel good about myself when we hung out together.

I wish that broken friendships would never happen, that fun times would never end. Thank You, God, that You will never move away or stop talking to me. Thank You that our friendship is always strong and will never end.

Amen.

Myself

Blessed is the one who trusts in the LORD.

PROVERBS 16:20

Dear God...

Do I act the same way regardless of who I'm with? Am I basically the same person at home as I am at church or at school? Or do I tend to change my personality and my actions depending on who I'm with and where I am?

It's natural to act a little bit different in different environments, but I should mainly be my true self all the time. I shouldn't ever try to be something I'm not just so I can be with a certain group or so people will think of me in a certain way. And this includes my online, social media self as well as my real, in-person self. God, You made me to be who I am, and I should be proud of myself—no matter who I'm with or where I am.

Amen.

Impact

Walk with the wise and become wise,
for a companion of fools suffers harm.

PROVERBS 13:20

Dear God...

I want to make my world a better place. One of the biggest ways I can do that is through my friendships. And just as I can have a big impact on my friends, my friends can have a big impact on me.

That's why I need to choose my friends carefully and really consider what makes a good friendship. Lord, please help me not to become so worried about status or popularity that I sacrifice the things that really matter in a friendship, like serving and being kind and listening. Most of all, help me to share my heart for You with my friends. That makes a bigger impact than anything else.

Amen.

Example

Do not be misled: "Bad company corrupts good character."

1 CORINTHIANS 15:33

Dear God...

When I was little, most of my friendships were chosen for me. The kids who were in my playgroup. The other girls in my beginning ballet class. The children in my preschool class. As I get older, I have a lot more say in my friendships. Every year I add to the list of people I know, which means way more potential friends to choose from.

Jesus, help me choose the right kind of friends—friends who make good choices, friends who are kind, friends who follow You. Friends who are a good example to me. Also give me godly mentors—older friends who will show me how to make right decisions and walk in Your ways. Bring these people into my life so I will have an easier time following You.

Amen.

Change

*I praise you because I am fearfully and
wonderfully made;
your works are wonderful,
I know that full well.*

PSALM 139:14

Dear God...

I have a lot of layers. There's the me who likes
to be silly with my friends, and there's the me who
likes to sit on my front porch swing and quietly
get lost in a book. There's the me who likes adventure
and exploring, and there's the me who likes to
spend hours decorating my room. I'm interesting
and unique and...well, I'm *me*.

At times, though, I try to be like other people so I
will fit in. I downplay a part of who I am. I pretend to
enjoy something so I don't stand out. These changes,
though, actually make me less interesting. Less
unique. Less *me*. Lord, You made me who I am. Help
me to embrace this and change only when I know I
should change—when You want me to change.

Amen.

Always

*The LORD himself goes before you
and will be with you; he will never
leave you nor forsake you. Do not
be afraid; do not be discouraged.*

DEUTERONOMY 31:8

Dear God...

My friendships seem to come and go. One day I feel like I have tons of friends, and the next day I feel all alone. With just one or two friends absent from school, I can feel lost. When everyone leaves for summer camp or vacation, I'm on my own. And when my friends and I start having different interests and hanging out with other people, I can feel especially alone.

Even though my friendships are shifting and changing, I know that You are always with me. You are always faithful and will never leave me wondering, *Are we friends or not?* It's so nice to have that security, that reassurance that I always have someone to talk to. Always.

Amen.

Discernment

This is my prayer: that your love may abound more and more in knowledge and depth of insight, so that you may be able to discern what is best.

PHILIPPIANS 1:9-10

Dear God...

Sometimes I just get a feeling about something. I can tell deep down that a situation or a person isn't okay. I feel scared or anxious or nervous, and I can't always specifically say why I feel this way. I just do. The feeling is strong, and it doesn't go away.

There's a name for this feeling. *Discernment.* And I'm learning it's an important thing to have when I'm choosing my friends. Some people refer to it as getting a read on people. Some call it following your instincts. Lord, when it comes to my friendships, remind me to be careful. I become like the people I spend time with, and I need to find friends who will help me become stronger in who I am and stronger in You.

Amen.

Acceptance

Did God reject his people? By no means!

ROMANS 11:1

Dear God...

There's a group of girls who seem like they've been friends since birth. They know exactly what to wear and how to style their hair. They always look cool and sound cool and act cool. Everyone seems to look up to them, and everyone wants to be accepted by them.

God, I'll admit that I want to be part of that group. But the fact that they don't accept everyone proves they're not perfect. Actually, sometimes they can be pretty mean. To be honest, I know I'm not like them. I know they're not the best friends for me. I know there's only one kind of acceptance that matters—Your acceptance. And I already have that. Forever.

Amen.

Contentment

Godliness with contentment is great gain.

1 Timothy 6:6

Dear God...

Sometimes when I come home from my friend's house, I'm in a bad mood. Her house is so big. Her parties are amazing, and there is always so much food! There's no way my next birthday party will even come close to hers.

I hate it when I don't feel content, when I wish I had more. I also wish I didn't compare myself to my friends, but I do. I can't help it. Lord, help me see beyond what I don't have, and to focus on what I do have—siblings to play with, rooms filled with books and games, cuddly cats and delightful dogs. My family is special. My home is perfect for me. I have enough, and I'm content.

Amen.

Bold

Since we have such a hope,
we are very bold.

2 CORINTHIANS 3:12

Dear God...

Sometimes I'm considered the shy one in my group of friends. I'm not the girl with the loudest laugh or the quickest comeback. I'm the laid-back girl who always smiles and prefers to listen and think before I say something.

Because I'm this way, it can be hard for me to speak up when I notice something isn't right or needs to be done. But I don't need to be afraid to speak my mind or share what's on my heart. I shouldn't hesitate to be bold. I've earned the trust of my friends by being a good listener and a kind person, and they respect what I have to say. Lord, let my words be loud and clear and spoken with boldness and love.

Amen.

Good

A friend loves at all times.

PROVERBS 17:17

Dear God...

When I meet people, I notice their good sense of humor. Their fun fashion sense. Their impressive talents. But those aren't the things I should consider when I'm considering someone as a potential new friend. It's so easy to focus on the outside—how someone looks or talks or acts. It's harder to notice what's inside.

But what really counts is inside. I'd rather be friends with someone who is kind than someone who wears the latest fashions. I'd rather have a friend who makes me laugh than a friend who laughs at me. I'd rather have a friend who is good than a friend who is impressive. Lord, help me to take notice when a person is good on the inside. That is what will make our friendship strong.

Amen.

Actions

I can do all this through him
who gives me strength.

PHILIPPIANS 4:13

Dear God...

It's easy to spend a whole lot of time doing nothing at all—especially during summer vacation. My friends and I can spend hours and hours sending silly messages online or binge watching our favorite TV shows. We're not doing anything bad, but we're not exactly doing anything good either.

God, when I'm feeling stuck and bored, help me to take action. I can call up a friend and make a plan. Together we can clean our rooms or another part of the house. We can set up a lemonade stand for our younger siblings or start a babysitting business together. The best part is that we'll actually accomplish something—and have fun in the process. Friends who take action together grow together. We share memories. We become inspired. And with Your help, we can make a difference in our world.

Amen.

Comfort

Encourage one another and build each other up, just as in fact you are doing.

1 Thessalonians 5:11

Dear God...

When my friend's world falls apart, I don't know what to do. I make excuses for not going over to her house when everyone seems so upset there. I put off talking to her because I don't have the right words to say. I don't understand what's going on, and it seems easier just to avoid her.

But I know I need to be there for her. I need to share Your love with her, Lord. I need to be available in case she wants to talk—or just wants to spend time together in silence. I don't have to completely understand things or have the perfect words or a solution to the problem. Help me to pray and offer comfort, and that will be enough.

Amen.

Effort

*As iron sharpens iron,
so one person sharpens another.*

PROVERBS 27:17

Dear God...

Friendships take effort. As my friends and I start dealing with changing emotions, we hurt each other with our words more often than we used to. Ugly feelings like jealousy and mistrust and insecurity make a mess of our relationships.

It's inevitable that my friends and I will get into disagreements, but I need to do my part to make sure we get through the hard times and become better friends than ever. Help me learn how to communicate. How to say I'm sorry. How to just let some things go and chalk it up to a bad day. Most of all, remind me to pray about my friendships, Lord—that You will show me how to make the effort and teach me when to hold on and when to let go.

Amen.

Prayers About

Happiness and Contentment

Smile

*Light in a messenger's eyes
brings joy to the heart.*

PROVERBS 15:30

Dear God...

When I hear the word "contagious," I think of something I don't want to get. Colds are contagious. The flu is contagious. Chicken pox is contagious. But good things can be contagious too. Like happiness. Or a positive attitude. Or a smile.

God, help me to remember to smile even if I don't feel like it. My smile can turn someone else's rough day into a promising one—including my own. When someone smiles at me, my immediate reaction is to smile back. And just the act of smiling helps put me in a better mood. Sometimes, it really does help to fake it till I make it. But I actually don't have to fake it, Lord, because You always give me a reason to smile.

Amen.

Joy

*May the God of hope fill you with all
joy and peace as you trust in him, so
that you may overflow with hope
by the power of the Holy Spirit.*

ROMANS 15:13

Dear God...

When everyone around me is complaining, it's easy to find things that are wrong. The math assignment is too hard. The cafeteria lunch is disgusting. None of my clothes seem to fit right—and they're boring. It's easy to give in to negativity, especially when I'm surrounded by it.

That's why I need to practice finding joy in every moment and every situation. I need to treat it like a treasure hunt, seeking out spots of brightness and positivity in the gray. My math teacher is helpful. The cafeteria food isn't *that* bad. My clothes keep me warm—and I'm going shopping for new shoes this weekend. Best of all, I don't have to rely on *things* to bring me joy. You live in my heart, so joy is always present in my life.

Amen.

Gratitude

*Give thanks in all circumstances; for this
is God's will for you in Christ Jesus.*

1 Thessalonians 5:18

Dear God...

When I'm struggling to find things to be thankful for, help me to take action. To figure out a plan. To come up with a solution. This verse tells me that You want me to praise You in everything, so I need to find a way to make this work.

I can keep a little notebook by my bed—a gratitude journal or a book of thanks—and write down the things I'm grateful for as they come to mind. I can share things I'm thankful for at the dinner table with my family. I can include the things that make me happy and content when I'm talking to You. The method doesn't matter, but the action does. Please help me to always have a plan in place for practicing gratitude.

Amen.

Silly

You make me glad by your deeds, LORD;
I sing for joy at what your
hands have done.

PSALM 92:4

Dear God...

When I was little, I liked to dress up, play make-believe, have my hair done in funny styles, and dance all around the room to silly music. I was never unhappy when I was acting like this—not a care in the world—and I need to remember this feeling.

As I'm growing up, it's still okay for me to be silly, isn't it? It doesn't matter how I look as long as my heart is happy and I'm having fun. I just need to turn up the music and dance. I can even have a family member or a friend join me. Everyone needs moments like these! Thank You, Jesus, that I'm never too old to have happiness in my heart, and thank You for giving me permission to be silly.

Amen.

List

If we know that he hears us—
whatever we ask—we know that
we have what we asked of him.

1 JOHN 5:15

Dear God...

It's easy to get stuck in a rut when I'm trying to pray. I find myself repeating the same words and ideas over and over again. And honestly, that's when prayer gets kind of boring and I feel like giving up. Instead of giving up, though, maybe I need to shake things up.

I can grab a notebook or piece of paper or even my phone and start making a list. Ten things I'm thankful for. Five people to pray for. Three situations I'm unsure about. Even one hundred awesome things about You and Your creation. The number doesn't matter. Spelling doesn't count. Or handwriting. I just need to be honest and truthful in talking to You, God. And I can do this in a new and creative way by making a simple list.

Amen.

Good

You are good, and what you do is good;
teach me your decrees.

Psalm 119:68

Dear God...

I've heard the expression a million times—"It's all good." People say it in response to just about everything, and usually it's said as a positive end to the conversation. As in, no worries. It's not going to be a problem. It's all good.

Sometimes I feel like this is what You are saying to me. "Don't worry. I won't let this be a problem. I've got this. It's all good." Having an "it's all good" attitude means I don't have to compare myself to others. It means I don't have to worry about not being included by a certain group. It means I don't need to be anxious about going away to summer camp. You say it is good, and so I will keep telling myself those three comforting words: "It's all good."

Amen.

Humor

He will yet fill your mouth with laughter
and your lips with shouts of joy.

JOB 8:21

Dear God...

I cringe when I think about embarrassing situations. Some happened a year ago, and some happened last week. Even though I try to block them out of my mind, I can still recall the details. In full color. Like they just happened. And I'm freaked out about when something like that might happen again.

God, help me to laugh at myself when humiliating things happen. That would be better than trying to take the attention away from myself. Build in me a sense of humor that says, "Hey, this is no big deal. It's actually pretty funny!" Father, You have given me a sense of humor for a reason. You have a sense of humor. Thank You for reminding me that laughter is good for the heart.

Amen.

Imagine

*We are God's handiwork, created in
Christ Jesus to do good works, which
God prepared in advance for us to do.*

EPHESIANS 2:10

Dear God...

One of the greatest gifts You have given me is
my imagination, and I should never be afraid to use
it. Imagination brings beauty and goodness and
creativity to the world, and everyone does this in
her own unique way.

What are my gifts and talents, Lord? How can
I use my imagination to show Your awesomeness
and magnificence to the world? I can be an artist in
so many ways. I can write words of love and grace.
I can paint or draw images that celebrate creation.
I can dance or sing or play an instrument for Your
glory. So many possibilities. Please help me to use
my imagination to show the world Your goodness.

Amen.

Downtime

My Presence will go with you,
and I will give you rest.

EXODUS 33:14

Dear God...

There's a difference between having downtime and wasting time. This is something I see happening with my parents and older siblings. They work so hard at their jobs or studies, and they reach a point where they just need to stop and rest.

Help me to remember this, Lord, when I want someone to drive me somewhere or do something with me. They're not saying no because they don't want to be with me. They just need some downtime to refresh themselves and relax. As I get older, show me healthy ways to have downtime for myself—reading a book, taking a brief nap in a hammock, hanging out with a pet. Thank You for creating a time to work and a time to play—and a time to relax.

Amen.

Together

*With one mind and one voice you
may glorify the God and Father
of our Lord Jesus Christ.*

ROMANS 15:6

Dear God...

There's a lot of competition in my world. Who is the fastest runner on the team? Who is the smartest kid in the class? Who has the nicest clothes or the biggest house? Some kinds of competition can be good and push me to work harder and do better, but other kinds of competition aren't helpful at all.

When all is said and done, most things are better done together. Because if we're not helping each other, we're hurting each other. Or at least making each other feel bad or maybe even just a little bit sad. I may be the fastest runner, but I still need to encourage others. I can bring others up with me, just as they can bring me up with them. Together. That's how You created us to live, Lord—together in unity.

Amen.

Wonder

Let the little children come to me, and
do not hinder them, for the kingdom
of heaven belongs to such as these.

MATTHEW 19:14

Dear God...

You talk about little children in Your Word. And
You have such good things to say about them. Children were drawn to You, Jesus, and You praised
their openness to all You had to teach them. You
spoke of their sense of wonder and of their attitude
that was so wide open to believing Your message.

Thank You for creating me with this same sense
of wonder—please help me never to lose it. Because
along with that sense of wonder comes an openness to learning all You desire to teach me. I'm so
glad that You take everyone seriously—no matter
what her age is—and that You share Your same
message of love and grace with everyone.

Amen.

Prayer

Is anyone among you in trouble?
Let them pray. Is anyone happy?
Let them sing songs of praise.

JAMES 5:13

Dear God...

Sometimes I think that prayer is for bad times only. In fact, that's how I tend to pray. I pray when I'm scared or angry or uncertain. And I *should* pray in these moments. But I should also pray when times are good.

When life is going really well, I should keep praying. Keep talking to You. Keep telling You my hopes and dreams and feelings. When I am celebrating what is good in my life, I need to share that with You. When I have great new opportunities or have accomplished something big, I need to tell You what's going on. Please remind me to pray every day of my life, in the good times as well as the bad.

Amen.

Prayers About
My Worries

Comfort

May your unfailing love be my comfort,
according to your promise to your servant.

PSALM 119:76

Dear God...

I can think of lots of things I want when I'm feeling hurt or scared, but probably the number one thing I want is comfort. I want someone to hold my hand or rub my back and tell me that everything is going to be okay. My trial might be a scraped knee or a fear of the dark, or it might be much bigger than that. But no matter what it is, I need comfort.

It's so comforting to know that You are always there for me, God. You wipe away my tears. Your peace overcomes my worry. Your security replaces my fear. You hold my hand and reassure me that it's all going to turn out okay. Thank You for comforting me.

Amen.

Unknowns

When I am afraid, I put my trust in you.

PSALM 56:3

Dear God...

Sometimes I skip to the end of a book to see how it's going to turn out. I'm just way too curious about the situation or the characters, and I don't want the story to be a mystery to me anymore. I *need* to know what happens.

Sometimes I wish I could skip over some pages in my life. Is that friend drama I'm dealing with going to turn out okay? Are my family's problems going to be resolved in a good way? Are we going to end up moving to a new state, or am I going to be able to stay in the same house and attend the same school?

I'm glad You are here with me through the unknowns, Jesus. Thank You for being the author of my book.

Amen.

Slowly

Listen to my prayer, O God,
do not ignore my plea;
hear me and answer me.

PSALM 55:1-2

Dear God...

Sometimes I get tired of hurrying. Timed tests. Clocks running at soccer and basketball games. Bedtimes and early morning alarms. That ticking clock can sometimes freak me out! I get anxious about my test or my game or even about getting enough sleep and being tired the next day.

Jesus, when the clock seems to be ticking faster and faster, help me to slow down and focus on You. When I'm feeling anxious and like I'm running out of time, direct my attention to what is important in Your eyes. Keep my attention on what You want me to focus it on this day, this moment. Remind me that I don't have to worry about the next day or even the next moment. You're ultimately the one turning the hands of time. Help me to slow down and remember this.

Amen.

Near

Come near to God and he
will come near to you.

JAMES 4:8

Dear God...

I like being a part of my family and a member of my friend group, but it's comforting to know I don't have to be a clone of anyone else. I can be myself. I don't need to think like my mom or act like my best friend even though we're similar in many ways.

I'm so happy I get to follow the unique path You have created for me, God. You ask only that I stay near to You, tuned in to Your leading and Your guidance. Help me to remember this when I'm worried about who I am and how I appear and what others might think of me. The only things that matter are that You created me in Your image and that You keep me near to You.

Amen.

Darkness

*The light shines in the darkness, and
the darkness has not overcome it.*

JOHN 1:5

Dear God...

When darkness falls and strange shadows dance against my bedroom walls, I'm tempted to pull the covers up over my head and hide from the world. I pray for sleep to come quickly because it's no fun to lie awake in the quiet with my imagination running wild.

Jesus, You know I'm not just talking about being afraid of the dark. I'm talking about the many fears and anxieties that sometimes crowd my mind. I'm scared that my parents are arguing so much. I'm worried that my best friend stopped talking to me. I'm anxious that I keep getting sick and don't know why. Lord, You have given me Your promise that You will never leave me or forsake me. Thank You for comforting me in the darkness.

Amen.

Band-Aids

Heal me, LORD, and I will be healed;
save me and I will be saved,
for you are the one I praise.

JEREMIAH 17:14

Dear God...

It's the worst feeling to accidentally cut my finger and realize we're out of Band-Aids. Or to have a gigantic scrape and nothing big enough to cover it. The worst, though, is when I get a wound that a Band-Aid can't fix—when someone does something to me that just hurts and hurts and hurts.

Someone yells at me for no apparent reason. A kid at school makes fun of me in front of everyone. A girl who I thought was my friend makes up rumors about me and spreads them. These hurts are way too big for a Band-Aid and take more than a kiss to make them feel better. Lord, I give You all my hurts, and I trust that You will heal me in Your own time and in the best way possible—even if I can't find a Band-Aid.

Amen.

Stuffer

You will call on me and come and
pray to me, and I will listen to you.

JEREMIAH 29:12

Dear God...

Some people I know are stuffers. When something is wrong, they clam up and don't speak. When they're asked what's bothering them, they reply, "Nothing." Of course, it's not always a bad thing to stuff my feelings. I don't have to share every problem with everyone. I deserve some privacy when I just don't feel like talking.

But I need to make sure I'm not a stuffer when it comes to talking to You. I should never be afraid to speak my mind and my heart to You, Lord. When I bring my problems and feelings to You, my words need to be sincere and true. You will always listen and hear exactly what I am saying. It feels so good to know I don't have to hide anything from You.

Amen.

Stillness

Be still, and know that I am God.

PSALM 46:10

Dear God...

I'm not sure whether I'm an extravert (someone who never feels like she needs a break from people) or an introvert (someone who craves time alone), but I need moments of quiet and stillness. I need to be alone with my thoughts, to have time to wonder and pray.

Jesus, during Your ministry on earth, You were surrounded by crowds of people. A lot. And You always had patience with them, always seemed to know exactly the right thing to say. But even though You are the Son of God, You still took time away to be by Yourself. You still escaped the multitudes to hang out alone with Your Father. And so I too will seek rest from the craziness of the world—times of stillness, just me and my Father.

Amen.

Healthy

Praise the LORD, my soul,
and forget not all his benefits—
who forgives all your sins
and heals all your diseases.

PSALM 103:2-3

Dear God...

    Being sick is no fun. It doesn't matter whether I have a cold or the flu or a broken bone or any other kind of problem—basically, I hate feeling this way. I want to feel better immediately, but getting healthy usually takes some time.

    Jesus, I know that You are the great healer. You are the one who gives me health and strength and energy. I need to do my part—taking my medicine, getting enough sleep, drinking plenty of water—and allow You to work Your healing in Your time. Thank You that my family takes care of me when I'm not feeling well, and thank You for taking care of me too.

Amen.

Belief

Believe in the Lord Jesus, and
you will be saved.

ACTS 16:31

Dear God...

Life can be confusing. When I see bad things happen to good people or hear about scary things on the news, I get confused and don't know what to think. I want to believe that people are good and that the world is good, but the reality is that sin is a part of our world. And where there is sin, bad things happen.

Even if I can't understand everything going on around me, God, I can always rest in Your promises. You will never leave me. You will always love me. And in the end, You win. That's why I need to keep my belief strong—by reading Your Word, by talking to You, by doing my best to obey Your commands. That's how I strengthen my belief, and that's where I find my hope.

Amen.

Broken

The LORD is close to the brokenhearted.

PSALM 34:18

Dear God...

Sometimes I feel like my world is falling apart. Like when I received some really bad news and don't know how everything can be okay again. Or when things are a mess in my family. Or when my friendships are falling apart. One thing after another keeps happening, and I can get really scared about how everything is going to turn out.

But You specialize in the big stuff, Lord. All I need to do is look through the pages of the Bible and see how You can turn a situation around. When people felt like there was no way things were going to get better, You made a way and brought them to a place of peace and hope. Thank You that You are doing the same thing in my life—even in the big stuff.

Amen.

Choices

If any of you lacks wisdom, you should ask God, who gives generously to all without finding fault, and it will be given to you.

JAMES 1:5

Dear God...

Some choices are easy. Vanilla or chocolate. Book or movie. Swimming or biking. I know what I want—at least for that day—and I make my choice. I eat the chocolate ice cream cone. I read the book. I go for a bike ride.

Other choices are harder. Like my choice of friends. Or whether I want to quit the sport I've done for so many years and try something new. Or whether I should go along with what everyone else is doing even if I'm not sure it's a good idea. When I'm faced with a difficult decision, I need to spend time running it by You, Lord. And talking to others I trust. When I do this, I know You will help me make the right choice.

Amen.

Alone

*Cast all your anxiety upon him
because he cares for you.*

1 PETER 5:7

Dear God...

I want to be grown up and responsible and mature, but sometimes I'm just not up for that challenge. One of those times is when I have to stay home alone—especially when it's dark outside. I have a big imagination, and that's usually a good thing. Except when it's not.

Jesus, You are always with me, so I'm never really alone. Even in the darkness. It could be actual, literal darkness, or it could be the darkness of feeling alone in life. Sometimes I feel as if nobody understands me or nobody quite gets how I feel. But You created me, so You completely understand me. You totally get me. Even when it's dark out, Your light shines brightly in my life.

Amen.

Enough

*See what great love the Father has
lavished on us, that we should be called
children of God! And that is what we are!*

1 JOHN 3:1

Dear God...

One of my big fears in life is that I don't have enough. I don't have enough friends. I don't have enough stuff. I don't have enough brains or skill or talent. Other people always seem to have more—especially when I hear them talking about their grades or accomplishments or see the cool pictures they post online.

Lord, help me to realize that I don't always see the big picture. People don't like to talk about their failures or struggles. They don't post pictures where they look sad or just aren't doing much of anything. Everyone has moments when she feels like she doesn't have enough or just simply isn't enough. But I have You, Lord, so I have more than enough—and I *am* more than enough.

Amen.

Prayers About
My Life

Inside

*Your beauty...should be that of your
inner self, the unfading beauty of
a gentle and quiet spirit, which is
of great worth in God's sight.*

1 PETER 3:3-4

Dear God...

When I look at pictures of myself when I was a baby, I have to admit I looked pretty cute. Now, though, it's easier to find fault with myself. My skin isn't clear. My hair doesn't look the way I want it to. My clothes don't always fit the way I wish they would. I'm definitely not perfect.

But I know I'm becoming more and more perfect on the inside as I get to know You better and better. My beauty will become more radiant as I blossom in the care of Your perfecting love. And that's where I should spend my time and my energy—allowing You to improve me on the inside. What's in my heart is reflected in my actions and my attitude and even in my appearance. It's what's inside that truly matters.

Amen.

Created

God saw all that he had made,
and it was very good.

GENESIS 1:31

Dear God...

When I'm reading a book for school, I need to figure out the main point. What is the one big thing the author is trying to say? If I have this answer, I'll do well on the tests and assignments. That's because I get it. It makes sense to me.

The Bible is a huge book, and it can be hard to figure out. But here's the main message: You created me, and You want me to love You because You love me. When I remember these truths, everything else starts to make sense. How I'm supposed to think of myself. How I'm supposed to treat others. You created me and love me—once I get that, I'm on my way to living the life You created me to live.

Amen.

Worth

*Don't be afraid; you are worth
more than many sparrows.*

MATTHEW 10:31

Dear God...

It's easy to tell how much some things are worth.
A can of soda. A smartphone. A soccer ball. I figure
out what I want, and then I see about how much a
similar item sells for. If the price seems right, I buy
it, and it's worth the money I spend.

Because You love me so much, You didn't put
a price on me. I am worth everything to You, and
that's a pretty amazing thing. As the God of the uni-
verse, You can have absolutely anything because
You can make absolutely anything. And yet You say
I am priceless. When I start to wonder if I'm worth
anything at all, I need to remember this truth and
let Your love fill my heart.

Amen.

Clothing

She is clothed with strength and dignity;
she can laugh at the days to come.

PROVERBS 31:25

Dear God...

Sometimes when I look in the mirror, trying to decide what to wear for school, I get increasingly flustered. I try on one outfit and then another. Nothing looks right. The color is wrong or the fit is wrong or the style is wrong or...I just don't like it. Before I know it, it's too late even to eat breakfast. Not a good start to the day!

I can spend forever deciding what clothing to wear, but my time would be better spent determining what to wear spiritually each day. I need to put on the clothing of being a better friend or a nicer daughter or a more obedient student. And when I stand in front of the mirror that only You can see, Lord, I want to be clothed in compassion, kindness, humility, gentleness, and patience.

Amen.

Mirror

Those who look to him are radiant;
their faces are never covered with shame.

PSALM 34:5

Dear God...

It's so easy to compare myself to others. One friend doesn't have to wear braces—she gets to skip the pain and discomfort. Another friend seems naturally awesome at every sport she tries and doesn't know what it's like to struggle or to be picked last for teams. And another friend can read super fast and do hard math problems in her head. So not fair!

You don't want me to look in the mirror and see my (painful) braces or my frustration with sports or my struggle with certain school subjects. You want me to look in the mirror of Your love and to see what You see—a girl who loves her Lord, who is kind to her friends and family, who is doing her best every day.

Amen.

Security

Whoever dwells in the shelter of the Most High
will rest in the shadow of the Almighty.

PSALM 91:1

Dear God...

Sometimes I feel insecure. I'm not completely sure of myself. I question my abilities. I wonder who I am and what purpose I have. It's totally normal to sometimes feel this way. It can be hard to feel secure in a world of insecurity.

Because I have You in my life, Lord, I can be filled with confidence and security. And it's not because of me. It's because of You. Once I let go of the lie that it's all about me and accept the truth that it's all about You, it's easy to have confidence. It's simple to feel secure. When I take the focus off of myself, I experience a true sense of belonging.

Amen.

Different

*We have different gifts, according
to the grace given to each of us.*

ROMANS 12:6

Dear God...

It's amazing to me there are so many people in the world and yet I'm different from every one of them. Not that I do crazy things like dyeing my hair purple or wearing crazy clothes or listening to music nobody else has heard of. (I'm probably not allowed to dye my hair purple anyway even if I wanted to!) I'm just the only *me* on the whole planet.

Sometimes I want to stand out and say, "Hey, I'm my own person!" The good news is that You didn't make me like anyone else. You gave me my own looks, my own personality, my own uniqueness. Sure, I might share a first name with five other girls in my class or look super similar to my sister. But I'm *me*. And as long as I'm walking with You, the world is going to see my uniqueness as a very good thing, and I can be proud of being different.

Amen.

Exquisite

You created my inmost being;
you knit me together in my mother's womb.

PSALM 139: 13

Dear God...

When I look at a snowflake under a magnifying glass, I see that it is detailed and symmetrical and beautiful. It's *exquisite*. Every snowflake is a masterpiece created by Your amazingly talented hands. No two snowflakes are alike. Each one has its own unique structure.

I'm a pretty special snowflake too. Even You say so! Every work of Your hands is exquisite, perfect, and detailed. And that includes me. Sure, I'm not perfect. I make plenty of mistakes, and I will continue to make them. But because You never make mistakes, my life is not a mistake. And neither am I. You guide my path, and I celebrate that I am part of Your exquisite creation.

Amen.

Real

*Blessed are those who hunger and thirst
for righteousness, for they will be filled.*

MATTHEW 5:6

Dear God...

I see so many images on screens every day—photos posted on social media, images on TV, or YouTube videos. When I see these images, I need to ask myself an important question: Are these real? Is this the truth I'm actually seeing, or has this image been edited, and does the real thing actually look quite different?

Lord, when the images I see on screens are getting me down, please remind me to do something about it. I can turn the screens off. I can go outside or read a book or play with a pet. Do something real. Hang out with a friend face-to-face or spend time reading a devotional. There are so many wonderful things in life that are unedited and real. May I always have an appreciation and a hunger for these things.

Amen.

Trade

Be content with what you have.

HEBREWS 13:5

Dear God...

I'm just going to say it. Sometimes I wish I could trade places with someone else. My brother has my old swim coach—my favorite coach ever—and I wish I could switch places with him during practice. My best friend has her own bedroom while I share a room with my sister. I'd even love to trade places with my cat because she gets to sleep all the time!

You didn't make me someone else, though. You made me myself. You gave me my family and my home and my life for a reason, and You know what You're doing. Help me to remember this when I'm tempted to ask someone, "Hey, can I be you for a day? I'd love to trade places!" I can be content in all circumstances.

Amen.

Perfect

Whatever is true, whatever is noble,
whatever is right, whatever is pure,
whatever is lovely, whatever is admirable—
if anything is excellent or praiseworthy—
think about such things.

PHILIPPIANS 4:8

Dear God...

As I grow up, I feel more pressure to be perfect. Tests in school are more important than they used to be. My favorite activity—musical theater or a martial art or track club—is becoming more serious. Even my parents' expectations of what I do around the house and how I treat other people have reached a higher standard.

I usually just do my best, but sometimes I'm more concerned about being perfect than about having a good attitude. The end result—the A on the English test, the starring role in the musical theater production, the first place in the long jump—doesn't mean as much as the effort I put in to reach my goal. When a good attitude matches my good effort, I know I'll always come out ahead.

Amen.

Now

Trust in the LORD with all your heart
and lean not on your own understanding;
in all your ways submit to him,
and he will make your paths straight.

PROVERBS 3:5-6

Dear God...

When it comes to making good choices, I usually think of the big stuff that's way in the future—where I'll go to college, what job I'll have, whether or not I'll get married and have kids. These things are years and years away, but I tend to think that these are the important life choices and that the right-now stuff doesn't really matter.

It all matters, though—even the little things. Like developing a daily routine of brushing my teeth and washing my face. Eating nutritious food and getting enough exercise. Spending time reading my Bible and praying. Making the right choices in the everyday things will help me so much in my future. Even if it seems incredibly far away, it's coming. And I want to get ready for it now.

Amen.

Prayers About
Growing Up

Grace

*To each one of us grace has been
given as Christ apportioned it.*

EPHESIANS 4:7

Dear God...

I'm experiencing a lot of changes as I get older. Changes in my body. Changes in my emotions. Changes in my moods. Sometimes these changes are welcome, and sometimes, not so much. They can leave me feeling out of control and wondering whether I'll ever feel normal again.

It's good to know that everybody feels this way sometimes. Eventually my body and my emotions will sort themselves out and my roller coaster ride of moods will end. Until then, I need to remember that You give me lots of grace. So do my parents and my friends and the rest of my family—even though it doesn't always seem like it. And I can pass on that forgiveness and grace to others.

Amen.

Questions

Ask and it will be given to you;
seek and you will find;
knock and the door will be opened to you.

MATTHEW 7:7

Dear God...

It makes sense that the more I read and learn and study, the more answers I will have. But it seems to be the opposite. The more I live and learn, the more questions I have. What does it mean to be a good friend? How can I do my best in school? Why are some people so hard to deal with?

As I mature, life seems to bring more questions than answers. Fortunately, I have a source that holds all the answers—You. I like to know things for sure, to have a definite answer to my questions. Because I know You, I have access to the answers, kind of like a cheat sheet to life. All I need to do is stay close to You, and You will give me the answers to my many questions.

Amen.

Blessings

God is able to bless you abundantly,
so that in all things at all times,
having all that you need, you will
abound in every good work.

2 CORINTHIANS 9:8

Dear God...

I wonder what am I going to become some-day. What is my life going to look like when I'm all grown up? Where will I live, and what kind of job will I have? I have so many ideas about what I'd love to do someday and who I'd love to be.

Lord, I know that You want great things for me. You have promised to shower me with Your bless-ings, and I ask that You open my eyes to seeing and appreciating them. My idea of blessings might not quite line up with Your idea. And that's okay. You will continue to teach me. Your vision is clearer than my clouded expectations and ideas. I pray that my future will be filled with Your blessings—the riches of friends, family, and purpose.

Amen.

Transitions

Be strong and courageous. Do not
be afraid or terrified...for the LORD
your God goes with you; he will
never leave you nor forsake you.

DEUTERONOMY 31:6

Dear God...

Transitions can be tricky. Babies have trouble transitioning from playtime to naptime. Bath time to feeding time. Even the transition from the house to the car can be hard for some little ones. I probably had some challenges with transitions when I was a baby, but thankfully, I've outgrown my difficulty with these particular transitions. I learned how to deal with change in my life and even welcome it.

Even though I'm no longer a baby, I still face many transitions throughout the day. And I will continue to face many transitions as I mature. Some of these transitions are exciting. Others are difficult. They can even be difficult *and* exciting—at the same time! Throughout my many transitions, Lord, give me the courage to cling to You.

Amen.

Journey

Direct my footsteps according to your word;
let no sin rule over me.

PSALM 119:133

Dear God...

Sometimes I'm excited about growing up. But at other times I just want to go back to the life of coloring and dress-up and make-believe! I often feel caught in between on this journey. I'm no longer a little girl, but I'm not yet a woman. How am I supposed to act? What am I supposed to say and do?

I want to speak and act with conviction and confidence. As long as I am following You, I will have a good idea of what is right and what is wrong. And I will have the confidence to speak and act appropriately. I can still laugh and play and have fun, but I can be serious when I need to be and mature enough to make my voice heard on this journey.

Amen.

Growing

*Grow in the grace and knowledge of
our Lord and Savior Jesus Christ.*

2 PETER 3:18

Dear God...

I've been learning to figure things out for myself. I don't ask for help as much as I used to, and this is usually a good thing. Being able to take care of things for myself—from fixing a bike tire to making a simple meal—is a very good skill to have. And even if I don't do things perfectly the first time, the next time is always a little bit better.

At times, I can feel all alone as I figure out my way. But I can always ask someone for help when I'm stuck, and I will never really be on my own. Help me to feel my parents' love and Your love, God, as I move through challenges, difficulties, and accomplishments. I'm always learning and always growing.

Amen.

Experience

*Do not forget to do good and to
share with others, for with such
sacrifices God is pleased.*

HEBREWS 13:16

Dear God...

I might not think I have a lot of life history, but when I count up how many days I've been alive, I realize it's a pretty big number. I have seen a lot and done a lot and have a lot of great memories along with some things I wouldn't mind forgetting (hello, embarrassing moments!).

Even though I'm still a kid, my experience counts. I have good advice to give to others. If I have learned a lesson and You want me to pass that on, help me to do just that. Help me never to be down on myself because of my age. Or to think my experience doesn't matter. My contribution to this world is important—right now. Please remind me every day that I can make a difference.

Amen.

Time

*Do not worry about your life, what
you will eat or drink; or about
your body, what you will wear.*

MATTHEW 6:25

Dear God...

Sometimes I wish I could slow down time, and sometimes I wish I could speed it up. I love celebrating birthdays, but there's always a tiny bit of sadness that I won't ever be that age again. And New Year's Eve is so much fun, but the year that's fading into the past is filled with so many great memories.

It seems like I'm looking ahead a lot—to the next grade, to the next level of my sport, to the age when I'm old enough to get a phone or a laptop or something big and important. In the rush to get ahead, sometimes I forget about the joy and beauty of this very moment. Jesus, help me to be excited about the future but also to be content in the present.

Amen.

Invincible

*In Christ Jesus you are all
children of God through faith.*

GALATIANS 3:26

Dear God...

I used to spend my days dressing up and pretending to be a girl superhero or an adventurous princess. I thought of myself as invincible as I careened around corners and leaped over large pillows. Nobody was as strong or as brave or as beautiful as me!

I have a little secret. Sometimes I still pretend to be that superhero or that princess. I have the ability to save whatever needs saving. I can overcome any obstacle and meet any challenge. And I'm determined to hang on to that little kid part of me that is fearless and amazing. After all, that's how You think of me, God—as Your princess, as Your superhero in training.

Invincible...that's me!

Amen.

Distractions

*I am saying this...that you may
live in a right way in undivided
devotion to the Lord.*

1 Corinthians 7:35

Dear God...

When I get distracted, my parents or my teachers say, "Look at me when I'm talking to you." Sometimes what's happening outside the window seems so much more interesting. Or I'm thinking of a book I just read or a movie I just watched.

Life is full of distractions, and I need to keep them from getting in the way of my paying attention. When I'm supposed to be listening to my teacher in school, please help me to stay focused. When my mom or dad is talking to me, help me to be present. When my friend is sharing her problems with me, help me to tune in. And when You are speaking to me, God, help me to be aware. Ignoring distractions takes practice, but I know I can do it with Your help.

Amen.

Trends

*Jesus Christ is the same yesterday
and today and forever.*

HEBREWS 13:8

Dear God...

When I think back to a trend that was popular one or two years ago, it seems like at the time everyone was following it. But is anyone following it now? No way! Trends and fascinations capture everyone's attention and interest, but they can fade away pretty fast.

It can be exhausting to keep up with trends, and that's why I'm glad some things in my life are always consistent. You are one of those things. You're not suddenly "in" or "out," and You don't care if I'm "in" or "out." Trends come and go, but You are always consistent. Please help me to remember this when I'm spending time worrying about fitting in and following the crowd.

Amen.

Resist

*Blessed are the pure in heart,
for they will see God.*

MATTHEW 5:8

Dear God...

Sometimes I need to resist—to push back or go against something. For example, I want to resist the trend to grow up too quickly. I see girls younger than me wearing makeup and clothes designed for someone much older. And they act a certain way too—much older than they are—to try to get attention.

I've had friends try to grow up too quickly, and it's hard on our friendship. But this doesn't mean I need to join them in their actions or behavior. I can keep being myself and doing what is comfortable for me and what my parents allow. There's absolutely nothing wrong with this. In fact, there's everything *right* with this. Thank You, God, for helping me to resist the world and to feel confident in doing so.

Amen.

Plan

The plans of the diligent lead to profit.

PROVERBS 21:5

Dear God...

Sometimes I lose track of what's happening when. I thought my science project was due next week, but it's actually due in two days—oops! And I have a softball game tonight, and tomorrow night my family is going out for my mom's birthday. If only I had paid attention when my teacher announced when the science projects were due...and if only I had written it down somewhere.

As I get older and have more and more things to do, please help me to get into the habit of planning. That includes paying attention to what's happening when and writing things down on a calendar or in a notebook. When I have a plan, I'm a lot less stressed. And I'm able to give my best to the things that matter most.

Amen.

Becoming

*[Sing] to God with gratitude
in your hearts.*

COLOSSIANS 3:16

Dear God...

Looking in the mirror, I can see a glimpse of who I am becoming. But some things remain a mystery. Will I stay short, or will I grow taller? Will my hair stay light, or will it darken? What will I look like without my glasses or braces? Who is the future me, and would I recognize her if I saw her walking down the street?

I don't have a lot of control over what I will end up looking like on the outside, but I do have control over who I'm becoming on the inside. Am I becoming kinder? Am I becoming more loving and helpful? Am I becoming closer to You? When it comes to growing up, it's the inside that I need to spend the most time on. Please help me to always make that my priority, Lord.

Amen.

Prayers About
My Future

Risk

Look to the LORD and his strength;
seek his face always.

1 CHRONICLES 16:11

Dear God...

I love that feeling of finally doing something I've been super terrified to do. Like dive headfirst into the pool the first time. Or get up enough courage to finally ride that roller coaster. Or sing a solo in church. And once I've done that scary thing for the first time, suddenly it's not so scary anymore. In fact, it's actually fun!

That's the way You want me to live my life, God. Taking risks. Trying new things. Seeking adventure. Being open to whatever plan You have for me. You have some amazing stuff on my to-do list, and You're excited about my future. Taking Your risks might be scary at first, but it's so worth it. And the more I say yes to You, the more incredible my life will be.

Amen.

Adventure

*Those who know your name trust in you,
for you, LORD, have never
forsaken those who seek you.*

PSALM 9:10

Dear God...

When I hear the word "adventure," I think of something big. Like climbing Mount Everest. Or swimming across a stretch of the ocean. Or backpacking around the world. Adventure implies something that seems almost impossible to do.

Even if I don't climb Mount Everest or swim in the ocean or backpack around the world, You still have a life of adventure planned for me. Maybe my life will be spent as a missionary or a mom, a scientist or a singer. Maybe I'll end up doing all those things! When it comes down to it, though, anything can be an adventure. I can't know for certain what I'll become when I'm grown, but I *can* see the future as a gift—the gift of adventure—and I can choose to follow You, God.

Amen.

Gifted

Each of you should use whatever gift
you have received to serve others.

1 PETER 4:10

Dear God...

Some girls seem to know right away what they're really good at. One of my friends is an amazing artist. Another is incredible with animals. And yet another writes the most awesome stories and poems. Me? I'm not so sure yet.

Instead of getting discouraged and wondering whether I'm gifted or talented at anything, I need to keep trying new things until I find my thing. Maybe I actually have a number of things that are my thing, and I just haven't discovered them yet. But I will. God, You promise that You will show me. Until then, my job is to keep learning and trying and growing. You formed me, Lord, and my identity is in You. That alone makes me a gifted girl!

Amen.

Passion

I trust in your unfailing love;
my heart rejoices in your salvation.

PSALM 13:5

Dear God...

I'm passionate about my pursuits. I take on a task of interest and pour my heart and soul into it. When I'm loving something, I'm all in. I want to keep creating and exploring and learning. I can never get enough!

Lord, thank You for making me this way. I'm excited to see what my future holds. What passions will be part of my future, I wonder? What will You give me to spark my imagination, energy, and diligence? I pray that I will always have a heart that hungers for You and Your wisdom, God. And I also pray that my passions and pursuits will always serve You in the days and years to come.

Amen.

Wants

Take delight in the LORD,
and he will give you the
desires of your heart.

PSALM 37:4

Dear God...

My Christmas or birthday wish lists can be about a mile long. Once I begin writing down a few things I want, I just keep adding to the list. I want...I want...I want. All that wanting doesn't take into account what someone else might want to give me though.

Sometimes I want things that are beyond my reach, beyond my needs, and beyond what someone else—like You, God, or my parents—might want for me. When I find myself dissatisfied with what I have and what I've been given, that's a good time for me to stop wanting things for myself and to ask myself a few questions: What do You want for me? And what do I want for others? Please help me to align my wants with Your wishes for me.

Amen.

Purpose

"I know the plans I have for you,"
declares the LORD, "plans to prosper
you and not to harm you, plans
to give you hope and a future."

JEREMIAH 29:11

Dear God...

When I realize that You have a plan and a purpose for my life, I get pretty excited! It's so cool to think of You making a list of amazing things for me to do. And it's cool to imagine myself doing those things.

It can be easy to get so caught up in looking ahead at my future, though, that I forget about You. Your plan and Your purpose for me are nothing without You. I need to think of my life as a group project between You and me, God. When I mess up the plan, You are there to pick me up and get me going again. When I can't see the next step, You will guide me. Together, You and I can accomplish amazing things, and I can live out my purpose.

Amen.

Hope

Be strong and take heart,
all you who hope in the LORD.

PSALM 31:24

Dear God...

Sometimes I think, *I hope I can do this.* Or *I hope I can get that.* Or *I hope everything works out.*

I hope for a lot of things in my life. If I didn't have hope, what would I have? Hope gives me a positive attitude. Hope pushes me to keep trying. Hope shows me that there's always a way forward.

The important thing is that I place my hope—and my trust—in You, God. Even though friends and family and teachers help me and guide me, ultimately You are the one who gives me hope. You shine Your hope into my life and along my path, God. When I'm discouraged or disappointed, I can turn to You for a refill of hope. And then I believe...*I can do this. I can get that. Everything will work out!*

Amen.

Overwhelmed

I trust in you, LORD;
I say, "You are my God."

PSALM 31:14

Dear God...

There are days when I wish I could just push a pause button on life. Too much homework! Too much friend drama! And way too many chores! Doesn't anyone understand that I'm feeling overwhelmed? I can't possibly do everything for everyone and be everything to everyone. I just need a break!

Actually, taking a break when I'm feeling overwhelmed is a very good idea. Stopping for five or ten minutes to pray and think and be refreshed may seem like an odd thing to do when I am trying to get more stuff done, but it will do wonders for my attitude. When I've quieted my heart, I think more clearly. God, help me to push pause sometimes—and then to return to my tasks or my conversations with a new outlook, ready to take on the world once again.

Amen.

Priorities

Show me your ways, LORD,
teach me your paths.

Psalm 25:4

Dear God...

I feel like I have a lot going on—schoolwork and activities and hobbies...My efforts are divided by many loyalties. I want to say yes to everyone and do my best at everything. I don't want to let anyone down. I don't want to let myself down. And I don't see this getting any easier in the future.

Jesus, when I'm feeling like I have way too many important things going on in my life, help me to prioritize them. Show me what should come first. Give me a heart that makes the best thing my priority, and show me what that best thing is. And also show me how to best follow Your leading.

Amen.

Continue

*Show this same diligence to the
very end, so that what you hope
for may be fully realized.*

<small>HEBREWS 6:11</small>

Dear God...

It's so easy to put down my math book and pick up the novel I'm reading or turn on my favorite TV show. Before I know it, an hour or two has gone by and I'm nowhere near finished with my math homework.

When I need to get stuff done—like homework or chores or even just-for-fun things—please help me continue until I finish. This is such an important lesson for me to learn. I want to deepen my relationship with You, Lord, so help me continue to pray. Continue to read my Bible. Continue to listen to Your voice. Help me develop the discipline and the willingness to continue, God, and show me the rewards of my hard work.

Amen.

Time

*Seek first his kingdom and his
righteousness, and all these things
will be given to you as well.*

MATTHEW 6:33

Dear God...

When I have a big test or assignment coming up, it's easy to skip my daily Bible reading. When I have a busy weekend schedule of sports or performances or birthday parties, it's tempting to ask if I can sleep in on Sunday and miss church. When I would rather watch one more episode of my TV show, it's easy to skip my nightly prayers.

Being with You, Lord, is the best way to spend my time. And the habits I form when I am young will stay with me for the rest of my life. Help me to remember this when I'm tempted to skip reading my Bible, going to church, or praying. Because without You in my life, nothing else really matters. The best kind of time is time spent with You.

Amen.

Persevere

Well done, good and faithful servant! You have been faithful with a few things; I will put you in charge of many things. Come and share your master's happiness!

MATTHEW 25:21

Dear God...

It can be hard to see the difference between stubbornness and perseverance. They have a lot in common, but the fruits they bear are so different. Stubbornness is when I dig in and refuse to see any other way to accomplish something. I want to do it *my* way. Perseverance is when I keep going despite problems and challenges. I persevere because I know the end result will be good.

Lord, help me to let go of my stubborn attitude and instead to adopt an attitude of perseverance. And help me to realize that perseverance is something I can't do right without You. I depend on Your strength to carry on. When I persevere, I stick with something and learn and grow in the process. What a terrific life lesson!

Amen.

Joy

You make known to me the path of life;
you will fill me with joy in your presence.

PSALM 16:11

Dear God...

Joy seems to be that thing I find at the end of my efforts. Getting first place in my swim meet. Dancing the role of Clara in *The Nutcracker*. Winning a blue ribbon at my horse show. I equate joy with applause and accolades and awards.

If I'm looking for joy only at the end of my efforts, though, I miss all the joy in the process. I miss the joy of training with my friends and perfecting my technique. I miss the joy of messed-up moments at rehearsals and the satisfaction of finally figuring things out. I miss the joy of being free to ride and ride and ride my favorite horse in the world. Jesus, show me joy in all the little moments. And help me pass that joy on to others.

Amen.

Why

Praise be to the LORD God, the God of Israel,
who alone does marvelous deeds.

PSALM 72:18

Dear God...

As a tiny toddler, one of my favorite words was "why." Why do flowers grow? Why are my eyes brown? Why does the rain fall? Even if I didn't understand the explanation I received, it didn't discourage me from asking why.

As I get older, my questions change, but I still find myself asking why. Why are my parents so strict? Why are my friends having so much drama? Why do bad things keep happening in the world? God, I know You want me to ask You why. I trust that You will answer my questions and show me Your plan and Your purpose in the midst of everything that is happening. Thank You for welcoming every question—even the ones that seem impossible to answer. I'm glad I can keep asking why.

Amen.

Prayers About
My World

Plenty

The generous will themselves be blessed.

PROVERBS 22:9

Dear God...

My Sunday school teacher passed out treats in class today. Quickly we all fell in line to receive our prize for memorizing verses—a super delicious cupcake. The kid at the front of the line passed the treat to the next and so on until everybody had one. All of us knew we would receive a treat, so we easily released the box of cupcakes to the next person in line without worry.

Your love is like that box of cupcakes, Lord. There's plenty to go around. When I remember this, I am willing and eager to pass along love to those I encounter. Lord, please give me a heart that overflows with the sweetness of Your love. And give me the desire and the patience to pass it on.

Amen.

Selfless

*Each of you should give what you
have decided in your heart to
give…for God loves a cheerful giver.*

2 CORINTHIANS 9:7

Dear God…

Sometimes I sound like the seagulls in *Finding Nemo.* "Mine, mine, mine." When I want something or I'm afraid there won't be enough of something, I focus on getting it for myself. That sounds a lot like selfishness, doesn't it, God?

If the opposite of selfishness is selflessness, then I want to have a selfless attitude. I don't want to be the kind of person who thinks I'm more important than others. I want to be able to say, "Here, this is for you." And I want to mean it. There are so many advantages to being selfless and so many disadvantages to being selfish. God, help me to put other people's needs before my own needs and to practice living a selfless life.

Amen.

Belonging

As the deer pants for streams of water,
so my soul pants for you, my God.

PSALM 42:1

Dear God...

Try as I might, I can't avoid getting hurt in life. I hurt when I feel like I don't belong. I want to feel like an important part of a group or a team or a club, but sometimes I feel like I don't fit in. And maybe that's okay. Maybe I don't fit in because the rest of the group makes wrong choices or has different values. Maybe I don't fit in because You have something different planned for me—something better.

Lord, help me to remember that You are the only thing that will quench my thirst for acceptance and belonging. No friend will do that for me. Nobody else can offer the unconditional and unrelenting and totally satisfying sense of belonging that You offer to me. Please satisfy my thirst for belonging with Your mercy and grace.

Amen.

Serving

God is not unjust; he will not forget
your work and the love you have
shown him as you have helped his
people and continue to help them.

HEBREWS 6:10

Dear God...

It's fun to eat at a fancy restaurant where the water is poured for me and I don't have to set the table or wash the dishes. I don't get served like that every day, so I really appreciate it when I do. And maybe I ask to go out to eat more than I should!

Being served makes me happy, and when I serve others, it makes them happy. In addition, when I serve others I'm also serving You, Jesus. Bonus! In fact, serving someone else makes three people happy—the person I'm serving, me, and You. Serving is just an all-around great thing to do. Help me to search out opportunities to serve others, Lord. And show me the many ways I can serve You.

Amen.

Praise

Sing praises to God, sing praises.

PSALM 47:6

Dear God...

I want to tell the world about the love I feel for You, but sometimes it just isn't the right moment to start singing a praise song or praying out loud. I can feel uncomfortable doing those things in public, but I can praise You in other ways.

I can praise You by making a watercolor picture of Your creation. I can praise You by writing a poem about Your love. I can praise You by telling my friends about the awesome stuff You are doing in my life. There are so many different ways to praise You in this wonderful world. Whatever I'm doing or wherever I am, I will use my life to praise You daily.

Amen.

Empathy

*Blessed are the merciful,
for they will be shown mercy.*

MATTHEW 5:7

Dear God...

You are helping me become more mature in various ways. For example, You are giving me more empathy for others. I'm learning how to put myself in another person's place. To walk in her shoes. To feel what she feels.

Empathy helps me understand others. It also helps to keep me from getting hurt when a friend acts a certain way. I understand she's going through some hard stuff at home, and because I'm doing my best to put myself in her place, I can give her some grace and compassion and not take her comments too personally. Empathy isn't always easy, but it's definitely what You ask of me, Lord.

Amen.

Open

*Go into all the world and preach
the gospel to all creation.*

MARK 16:15

Dear God...

Am I too silent about my faith? Am I open about my belief in You? I want to live a life that points people to You.

Sometimes I feel You urging me to talk to my friends or classmates about You and what You are doing in my life—but I freeze up. I'm scared they will laugh at me or make fun of me or maybe even get mad at me. But please give me the courage and willingness to share and be open about my faith. The more people who come to know You, the better our world will be. Help me to be courageous and open and to allow You to share through me.

Amen.

Doing

The fruit of the spirit is love, joy, peace,
forbearance, kindness, goodness,
faithfulness, gentleness and self-control.

GALATIANS 5:22-23

Dear God...

There are so many ways to speak—talking out loud, texting, posting comments on social media, writing in a journal...I'm surrounded by words, words, words. So surrounded that I spend a lot of time worrying about what I say and forgetting that what I *do* is important too.

I might tell a friend who is sad, "Let me know if you need help!" and feel as if I actually did something. But wouldn't it be better to invite her over for ice cream or play a game with her or make her a card that says, "I hope you feel better"? In a world that's focused on screens and images and posted words, please remind me of the power of doing. Doing is often the best course of action. Doing can change the world.

Amen.

Letdown

I trust in your unfailing love;
my heart rejoices in your salvation.

PSALM 13:5

Dear God...

When there's a big buildup to something, there's always a letdown when it's over. So much preparation goes into celebrating Christmas—and then it's over. I spend hours and hours at soccer practice—and then the season ends. Even the end of the school year can be kind of a letdown when I find myself out of a routine and not seeing my friends as frequently.

It's not just situations that let me down. Sometimes people do, and being let down by other people can be really hard. Like when my friend promises to bring me on her family camping trip—and then invites another girl instead. When these letdowns happen, Lord, please give me the strength and character to depend on You and to rest in the assurance that You will never let me down.

Amen.

Connect

Love your neighbor as yourself.

MARK 12:31

Dear God...

I'm learning that the best way to make someone a friend instead of an enemy is to connect with her. To find something in common. To discover a shared interest—even if it's something silly, like a favorite Disney princess.

When I listen to others and focus on them, I find it easier to make connections. Making connections tears down walls. Even if I don't speak the same language as another person, I can still make a connection through smiles or laughter. God, what would happen if everyone in our world spent their energy connecting instead of comparing? I want to live in a world like that. Help me take the first step to making it happen by making connections.

Amen.

Patient

The LORD is good to those whose hope is in him,
to the one who seeks him;
it is good to wait quietly
for the salvation of the LORD.

LAMENTATIONS 3:25-26

Dear God...

I don't like it when others get in my way. I don't like slowing down to wait for a younger sibling or trying to explain the rules of a game to my dad. I just want to get on with my activity or my game and do things at my own speed.

But that's not how You want me to live my life, Jesus. You don't want me to barrel through a challenge, but to bear with another person. You care more about my relationship with my sibling or my dad than what I can accomplish on my own. You are patient with me when I'm slow to catch on or can't do something very quickly, so please help me to be patient with others.

Amen.

Fun

The heavens declare the glory of God;
the skies proclaim the work of his hands.

PSALM 19:1

Dear God...

You created the world for our pleasure, and You want us to have fun. You created lakes I can swim in. Trees I can climb. Mountains I can hike. And You also created me with energy and a thirst for adventure and fun.

Our world needs more fun, and I can do my part by playing. I can head out into nature on foot or on my bike. I can join my friends and family in playing games. When I immerse myself in playing and having fun, I forget about the things that don't really matter—like popularity or social media or what someone else said about me. I'm too busy having fun to care about those things, and I can be thankful for that.

Amen.

Beauty

The LORD loves righteousness and justice;
the earth is full of his unfailing love.

PSALM 33:5

Dear God...

The world says I can find beauty in lip gloss or a certain brand of clothing, but that's not true. Someday those things won't exist anymore, and then what? That kind of beauty doesn't last, and it's not true beauty anyway.

If I want to find true beauty, I need to look to You, Lord. I can see beauty in a sunset or the crashing waves of the ocean or a blanket of new snow. Even better, I can see the beauty You created in others—my grandfather's kind heart, my best friend's giant grin, my mom's crazy sense of humor. That is true beauty. Jesus, please help me cultivate true beauty in my own heart and life so I can help make the world a more beautiful place.

Amen.

Lovable

These three remain: faith, hope and
love. But the greatest of these is love.

1 CORINTHIANS 13:13

Dear God...

Some people just aren't very lovable. The girl who pulls my friends away and excludes me. The boy who makes fun of the way I walk. The grumpy uncle who just isn't nice. I have a hard time loving these people. Where is the good in them? Why do they act the way they do? How can I love them?

Sometimes all I can do is pray. And that's actually quite a lot. Lord, You promise to hear my prayers and be active in my life. And You love the world—the entire world and everyone in it. Including the excluding girl and the mean boy and the grumpy uncle. Please show me how to love these people, and please work in their hearts so that they understand how to love others too.

Amen.

Prayers About
My Walk with God

Disappointment

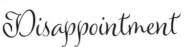

*The grass withers and the flowers fall,
but the word of our God endures forever.*

ISAIAH 40:8

Dear God...

Things don't always go the way I expect them to. I get sick on the day of my best friend's birthday party. Our family vacation to Disneyland has to be postponed. I'm not able to get a new puppy because we're moving. Life can be disappointing.

When one or two things go wrong, it's easy to start seeing problems everywhere. One disappointment after another. I forget to look for the good in every situation, and I sometimes miss the amazing things happening right in front of my face. Lord, please give me Your contentment—the kind of contentment that can handle disappointment and get me through problems big and small. Thank You for changing my outlook when I'm feeling down.

Amen.

Wholeheartedly

Love the Lord your God with
all your heart and with all your
soul and with all your mind.

MATTHEW 22:37

Dear God...

If I follow You with my whole heart, I know You will help me to love others wholeheartedly. To do my best work wholeheartedly. To embrace Your will for me wholeheartedly.

It's tempting to love my brother or do my homework or follow You halfheartedly. It's easy to put in the minimum amount of effort and just scrape by. As long as I do something, it doesn't matter how I do it, does it? Actually, it does. I should do everything to the best of my ability. Most of all, You want me to seek Your truth wholeheartedly. When I do this, You fill me with Your love and power and grace—and You give me the energy and strength to live life wholeheartedly.

Amen.

Walk

He tends his flock like a shepherd:
He gathers the lambs in his arms
and carries them close to his heart.

ISAIAH 40:11

Dear God...

When I was small and learning to walk, I would gradually let go of something—the couch, my mom's hand, the edge of the coffee table—and try to take a few steps on my own. Eventually I was able to walk by myself without holding on to anything at all.

That's kind of how it goes for most parts of growing up. I learn to walk by myself and navigate my world with less and less help. Except in one situation—my walk with You, God. When I'm walking with You, I actually need to hold on more and more. Whenever I let go of Your hand, I stumble and fall. Thank You for picking me up, dusting me off, and taking hold of my hand again.

Amen.

Graceful

*Grace and peace be yours in
abundance through the knowledge
of God and of Jesus our Lord.*

2 PETER 1:2

Dear God...

I've been thinking about the difference between being graceful and being full of grace. A ballerina is graceful, but is she always full of grace? Probably not—especially during rehearsal when her dance partner drops her and she snaps at him. A swan floating on a lake is graceful—until something makes it mad. Just because I can be graceful doesn't always mean I'm full of grace.

Lord, help me to remember this when I stumble. I try to do what is right and to be a good person, but I'm not perfect. And neither are others. When someone else hurts me or makes me feel bad about myself, help me to know how to give them grace. Because if I had to choose between the two, I'd rather be a girl filled with grace than a girl who is graceful.

Amen.

Mood

We praise you, God,
we praise you, for your Name is near;
people tell of your wonderful deeds.

PSALM 75:1

Dear God...

One of the best things I can do when I'm feeling moody is to turn on some happy music. Before I know it, I'm singing and dancing and feeling a whole lot better. I remember to be thankful for the good things You have given me, and I realize I really had no reason to be so grumpy.

How quickly I can transform my mood when I take action and make myself do something fun—like listening to happy music. I need only to sing, make music, and praise Your name, and my mood, my spirits, and my outlook are transformed. Help me to see that even in my moodiest moments, I always have a reason to sing and praise Your name when I'm walking with You.

Amen.

Reflect

Dear friends, let us love one
another, for love comes from God.

1 JOHN 4:7

Dear God...

It can be hard to know how to treat other people. Obviously, I'm not going to treat my best friend the same way I treat my volleyball coach or my elderly neighbor. But I can follow a basic rule: Treat other people the way You treat me.

God, You love me. You listen to me. You are patient with me. You are kind to me. And so much more! (I just need to read the Bible to find out everything else—and there's a lot of good stuff in there.) Help me to reflect to others the same treatment I receive from You. To show love. To listen. To be patient. And to be kind. When I follow Your lead, I'll always know how to treat others.

Amen.

Compromise

A hot-tempered person stirs up conflict,
but the one who is patient calms a quarrel.

PROVERBS 15:18

Dear God...

I like being right. I like winning arguments. I like knowing the correct answer. Sometimes, though, I like those things a little too much—like when an argument ends with me slamming a door or yelling at someone. And usually it's not about something life threatening or even life changing, even though I might feel that it is at the time.

I need to learn the art of compromise when it comes to things that don't really matter. Friendship should always come before being first—especially when my efforts to be first hurt the friendship. Lord, guide me to choose words and actions that breathe peace instead of conflict into a situation. Help me to know when to hold on and when I should let go. Help me to learn the art of compromise.

Amen.

Yes

I have chosen the way of faithfulness;
I have set my heart on your laws.

PSALM 119:30

Dear God...

When I was little, I said no all the time. I said it because I didn't know very many words, and it was a good way to express how I was feeling. When I was upset or sad or frustrated, I just stomped my foot and said, "No!"

Now that I'm older, I don't react the same way. And I tend to say yes more. But sometimes I need to say no. No, I'm not going to lie to my parents. No, I'm not going to help someone cheat on a test. No, I'm not going to talk back to the teacher. No, I'm not going to go along with someone else's bad choices. When I say no to doing bad things, I say yes to You, God. And yes to a life of obedience.

Amen.

Effort

*Whatever your hand finds to
do, do it with all your might.*

ECCLESIASTES 9:10

Dear God...

I know I'm supposed to work hard and do my tasks without complaining—homework, chores, practicing my instrument...But as long as I put in the effort, does it really matter what my attitude is like? After all, a little complaining never hurt anyone. Whining is no big deal. Letting out some dramatic sighs? Everyone does that!

And yet...my attitude affects my effort. If I start doing my math homework or practicing my trumpet or folding the laundry with a bad attitude, there's probably going to be something lacking in my effort. I'm going to be looking ahead to finishing instead of focusing on the task at hand. Lord, help me to see that my best attitude will produce my best effort.

Amen.

Whatever

Never be lacking in zeal, but keep your spiritual fervor, serving the Lord.

ROMANS 12:11

Dear God...

A lot of kids say, "Whatever." That one word says so much. *I don't care. It doesn't matter. I'm not really paying attention to what you're telling me.* That's what I'm saying when I respond, "Whatever." No wonder my parents and teachers and coaches get so annoyed when they hear kids say that word.

Sadly, I live in a *whatever* world—especially when it comes to spiritual things. The world's response to Your commands—to love each other, to do the right thing, to put others first—is often *whatever.* Jesus, please help me to always care about other people and to always care about You. When I have my heart in the right place, my response will never be *whatever.* Because I do care. It does matter. And I am paying attention to what You're telling me.

Amen.

Cure

Give thanks to the God of heaven.
His love endures forever.

PSALM 136:26

Dear God...

When I'm sick or injured, I always wish there were an immediate cure to my illness. I wish I could eat a magic food that would make my runny nose go away. Or drink a magic drink that healed up my sprained ankle. Unfortunately, most things take time to heal. I can do things that help—like eating chicken noodle soup or putting ice on my ankle—but mostly I just need to wait it out.

When my heart is hurting and I'm feeling sad or upset or discouraged, there is an immediate cure. I can go to You in prayer, God. I can read Your Word and allow You to heal my heart and transform me. Thank You for Your healing work in my life.

Amen.

Present

We must pay the most careful
attention, therefore, to what we have
heard, so that we do not drift away.

HEBREWS 2:1

Dear God...

I know that to learn Spanish, I need to go to class. To become a better ice skater, I need to practice at the rink. To improve my singing, I need to go to choir rehearsal. If I want to do something well, I need to be present.

Lord, I also want to become a better believer. I want to grow closer to You and become more and more like You. I want to become the girl You have destined me to become. To do this, I need to be present. I need to spend time with You, reading my Bible, listening to my Sunday school teachers and youth group leaders, and spending time in prayer. Help me to always stay present and be aware of Your presence.

Amen.

MORE GREAT HARVEST KIDS
DEVOTIONAL BOOKS

A Girl After God's Own Heart Devotional

Draw closer to God, learn valuable life lessons, and build self-esteem with these heartfelt devotions from best-selling author Elizabeth George.

You're God's Girl!

These daily devotions written directly to your heart will help you discover God's truth—who He made you to be, how unique and special you are, and how you fit into your world. See yourself through His eyes and allow His truth to make a difference in your life. The *real* you, the *true* you, is amazing!

For Girls Like You

Wynter Pitts gives you a correct definition of yourself, opening your eyes to God's truth and the difference it makes in your life. Each daily devotion includes a prayer to help you apply the lesson.

Your Every Day Read and Pray Bible for Kids

You can discover God's Word for yourself while building a foundation of Bible truths that stay with you forever! This just-for-kids daily Bible provides the perfect trio of engaging, easy-to-understand narrative, delightfully detailed illustrations, and prayers to draw you closer to God.

· ·

To learn more about Harvest Kids books
or to read sample chapters, visit our website:

www.harvesthousepublishers.com

HARVEST HOUSE PUBLISHERS
EUGENE, OREGON

· ·